GW00501889

You Know You're a
Sports Fanatic
When...

Ben Fraser

Illustrations by Roger Penwill

summersdale

YOU KNOW YOU'RE A SPORTS FANATIC WHEN...

Summersdale Publishers Ltd
46 West Street
Chichester
West Sussex
PO19 1RP
UK

www.summersdale.com

Printed and bound in China

ISBN: 978-1-84953-167-2

Substantial discounts on bulk quantities of Summersdale books are available to corporations, professional associations and other organisations. For details contact Summersdale Publishers by telephone: +44 (0) 1243 771107, fax: +44 (0) 1243 786300 or email: nicky@summersdale.com.

To...

From...

Your idea of Sunday worship involves kneeling at the altar of your 50-inch plasma TV screen to watch *Match of the Day* (for the second time).

You can't wear your Olympic gold medal anymore, as the chocolate inside has melted.

You'd vote for Jonny Wilkinson in the general election if he were an MP.

The police ask to question you regarding the disappearance of the Muhammad Ali waxwork at Madame Tussauds.

You're nicknamed 'Statto' by your friends, on account of your astoundingly extensive sports knowledge.

You can simultaneously listen to the cricket on the radio and watch the rugby on your iPhone while in the home stand at your team's football ground.

You enter every sporting contest you can – including the ones held at your child's junior school.

Like David Beckham, you chose to name your child after the place it was conceived — though 'Brixton' doesn't seem to have the same ring to it...

You start a Facebook group called 'The Babes of Sky Sports News'.

You're so desperate to appear in front of the crowd at The Crucible that you have considered streaking.

You know the rules of fistball,
chess boxing and elephant polo.

You insist on a 'Come as your favourite piece of sports equipment' fancy dress party for your birthday.

Your email address is 'world's_greatest_sports_fan_in_the_world_ever_ever@sportsfans.com'.

You're popular at pub quizzes
– but only for the sports round...

Your neighbours complain to
the council after you paint
your house to look like
a dartboard.

You automatically say
'not out' after telling
someone your age.

You're determined to get married
at Wembley, even if you have to
remortgage your house to pay for it.

You secretly want to be a contestant on
Total Wipeout, but know you'll never
be taken seriously as a sportsperson
again if you go through with it.

Your armchair football commentary vocab includes 'My mum could do better than that', 'You great wet lettuce' and 'GOOOOAAAALLLL!'

Your idea of a quiet weekend involves a Friday-night water polo class and a Saturday half-marathon, followed by a relaxing Sunday kite-surfing session.

Your favourite MP3 playlist starts off with the theme tunes to *Match of the Day*, *Formula 1* and *Ski Sunday*.

You spend hours trawling through YouTube to see if you can spot yourself in the crowd at any of the big sporting events you've ever attended.

Your boxing gear doubles up
as cold-weather clothing.

You think sports officials are
even more evil than
traffic wardens.

You don't have an opinion on global warming, but will happily spend a day discussing the finer points of Ronnie O'Sullivan's cue control.

You spend over £100 a week at
JD Sports.

A nostalgic tear comes to your eye if you think of the legendary *Grandstand.* Gone but not forgotten.

You wear football socks even
with your business suit.

You applied to be on *Record Breakers* just to get close to Kriss Akabusi.

You practise your spin-bowling in your sleep (much to the annoyance of your partner).

You can tell the Williams sisters apart,
even if they play each other.

You never notice the front page of a newspaper, even if there's a war on.

You refer to your kids as 'the next Rooney' or 'a budding Sally Gunnell' even though they're still in Pampers.

Jimmy Savile says that he absolutely can not fix it for you to play in the US Open and 'would you please consider the matter closed'.

Radio 5 Live stop taking your calls. (They're tired of discussing the ins and outs of Gareth Southgate's penalty miss in Euro '96.)

You enjoy experimenting by combining different sports disciplines: anyone for five-a-side tennis?

You've got your eye on a nice trophy cabinet, though you have nothing to put in it (yet).

You think cauliflower ears
are sexy.

You believe there is a time and a place for sport: any time, any place.

You take your idea for a Steve Davis stationery range onto *Dragons' Den* (and are surprised when you receive a full round of 'no's).

You can't understand why you have again been overlooked for Sports Personality of the Year.

You recycle your old sports equipment into various household furnishings – you're especially proud of your shuttle-cock chandelier.

You find yourself saying 'You cannot be serious' in an American accent in response to anything you happen to disagree with.

You watch so much international sports coverage online you become fluent in eight languages, including Japanese.

Thanks to a certain cricketing legend who features on the advert, you only eat Shredded Wheat for breakfast.

You have 'personal best' times
for everything from making
a round of tea at work to
changing a nappy.

Your knowledge of opera begins and ends with Pavarotti in Italia 90.

Your favourite movies are *Fever Pitch*, *Chariots of Fire* and all the *Rocky* films (yes – even *Rocky III*).

You proudly display all of your sporting awards, no matter how old or trivial.

You give measurements according to well known sporting venues, e.g. about twice as big as Lord's, but not quite as long as the fairway on the fifth hole at Gleneagles.'

Your response is 'good to firm' if someone asks about the weather on your holiday abroad.

Your garden is subtly arranged to function as an all-purpose sports ground: washing line for a rugby goal, apple trees for goal posts and an empty hanging basket to practise your slam dunks.

You convince your friends to join you on a 'pub decathlon'. (Or a heptathlon for the lightweights.)

You set up an evening class to instruct footballers on how to expand their repertoire of goal celebrations.

You take it as a compliment if a police officer says you were behaving like a racing driver.

You have a bumper supply of Fox's Sports biscuits (though you never eat the ones that show your favourite sport).

You once punched the person
next to you after hearing the
bell for last orders.

You photoshop yourself winning the World Cup, the Ashes, Wimbledon and the Grand National.

Your weekly £10 spread bet takes priority over food, bills and water.

You get confused after your neighbours tell you to stop making a racket. You've never made a racket, but now you think of it, it is a good idea.

You know the offside rule inside out and pride yourself on the clarity of your explanation.

Your pets know not to disturb
you on Saturday afternoons.

You have an entire wardrobe for storing your vast collection of trainers.

You think Sue Barker deserves a medal for putting up with Phil Tufnell on *A Question of Sport*.

You are the chairman and
director of the David Gower
fan club.

You organise a day of 'Office Olympics' for a team-building activity at work.

You attempt to break the World Record for the most keep-ups with a jacket potato.

You congratulate your friend
if they tell you they are feeling
'a bit below par'.

You bore the rest of your family to tears by making them listen to your own full-length version of the classified check.

You always spend the first
three hours at work tweaking
your fantasy football team.

You're spotted on live coverage of the Tour de France running alongside competitors in your florescent-green mankini.

You think that Des Lynam
should be the next James Bond.

www.summersdale.com